SWEET NOTHINGS

Rory Waterman was born in Belfast in 1981, grew up in rural Lincolnshire, and lives in Nottingham, where he is Senior Lecturer in English at Nottingham Trent University. His first collection of poetry, *Tonight the Summer's Over*, was a Poetry Book Society Recommendation and was shortlisted for the Seamus Heaney Prize. His second, *Sarajevo Roses*, was shortlisted for the Ledbury Forte Prize for second collections. He is also the editor of *W.H. Davies, The True Traveller* and the author of several books on modern poetry.

Also by Rory Waterman, from Carcanet

RORY WATERMAN

Sweet Nothings

CARCANET

First published in Great Britain in 2020 by
Carcanet
Alliance House, 30 Cross Street
Manchester M2 7AQ
www.carcanet.co.uk

A CIP catalogue record for this book is
available from the British Library.
ISBN 978 1 78410 939 4

Book design by Andrew Latimer
Printed in Great Britain by SRP Ltd, Exeter, Devon

The publisher acknowledges financial
assistance from Arts Council England.

CONTENTS

I.

II.

SWEET NOTHINGS

I.

Simon Peter saith unto them, I go a fishing. They say unto him, We also go with thee. They went forth, and entered into a ship immediately; and that night they caught nothing.

JOHN 21.3 (KJV)

Nothing to do but work,
Nothing to eat but food,
Nothing to wear but clothes,
To keep one from going nude.

BENJAMIN FRANKLIN KING, JR.

'How big's a cubit? I don't believe it. It couldn't…'
I looked up from my half-crayoned boat of giraffes
and suchlike at Mrs Millson, who knew. 'You wouldn't!
And you're not the first to think like that', she laughed.
But when Canon Rodgers, whose name I was too small
to appreciate, next gave our school assembly,
they singled me out to read. The tiny hall
grew huge. I stalled on 'Testify', 'Pharisee':
which parts to stress? And then we had to sing:
Kiiiss my aaarse, Lord, kiiiss my aaaaarse,
the bigger boys behind me muttered, grinning.
I gawped out at the wet-bright trees and grass:
no Flood in our world. Now I'm a world away
nursing another beer. A parent's age.

I only discovered a couple of nights ago:
the film Paul's mum tried to hide was *The Bat People*,
scrambling to wallop pause when we barged in
to ask if we could play footy. And she said *No*
(it was raining) then *Pack it in barging about*

so of course we watched it later, when she popped out –
or some of it. For half an hour I sat
in fear of all the new fears my mind might shout
that night, or others: a wizened me retching

my last, then last, then last; my fingers stretching
as cold translucence is pistoned through my veins;
the blade behind me on each dark homeward lane.

HARRIER?

Deergrass and alder and rowan, and roe deer
strutting behind them, and wrens everywhere
yapping and hidden, and grass of Parnassus
spread, dull meadowsweet dead for the year:

lead your mind back and re-follow that trail
down from the fields and the fit, frit pheasants,
to loop past carr and the oil-slickened water
it hung in, retting, gouged through the front

as autumn was carving and taking off summer –
paler sun, sharper wind, too-soon dusk
reminding us we'd miles to go
and time was shortening. Years ago.

REAPING

'We need to test harder whether we can take a young 18- or 19-year-old out of their PlayStation bedroom, and put them into a Reaper cabin and say: "Right, you have never flown an aircraft before. That does not matter, you can operate this."'
      Air Marshal Greg Bagwell

18 or 19 – what was I doing then?
Well, one day, I biked here
to RAF Waddington's 'viewing point',

from where I saw no action –
called by the urgent Tornados
which had skimmed our village

shocking pliant heads
at intervals of my childhood,
and must have come from somewhere.

Runway approach lights have switched on
and point skywards at nothing
coming in. A pigeon. A slip of moon.

A screech owl would be too apposite.
But I saw one once a mile from here,
on Bloxholm Lane. It stalled a moment,

then beat on past the hedges
tall as houses, living its purpose
suddenly beyond range.

And who knows what they do
in a concreted cube two hundred yards
behind wires and warning signs,

or who does it – or why
an inch from where it would have died
a sandfly fills its nest?

Grasses by the road
dip like a million rods
to a million tiny catches. A saloon

half a mile off indicates
only to the clouding dusk,
slows to corner the perimeter

on a red route B road to home.
Nothing to do but follow
at a generous distance.

UNIVERSITY OF LIFE
(June – October 2003)

> *'You see, in this country are a number of youths who do not like to*
> *work, and the college is an excellent place for them.'*
>   L. Frank Baum, Ozma of Oz

i. Salad Days

You had to get a job to get your fun.
I blocked out half that summer, left half free –
but where to start? 'Go to an agency',
mum said, irritated. 'Like your pals.'

(*Pals?*) I worked the Show for NCP,
pointing lines of cars across a field,
collected my hourly rate of pay from each,
and daydreamed as I guided two strips, then three,

back to back to back. I missed day two.
And next week, at the salad factory
cutting peppers in two and peppers in two,
hair-netted, in a fridge the size of a hangar,

I daydreamed as I prepped (slice, bang out seeds,
push halves into the cold incessant course
of bobbing pepper-boats, repeat, repeat)
then slashed a lagging thumb with so much force

they sent me to First Aid, where I felt ill,
and got shown to a small room where I bled
into a bandage, beneath a clicking clock –
a Slight Wound smiling sadly on a bed.

ii. Then Removals

My prize was backpacking, still weeks away.
Each morning the depot filled with pliant men,
grew hot with sweat, farts, smoke and Nescafé.

And yes, I wish that what I had to say
was *They were great, I fitted in as well*
(I came from a council house) but anyway

civics, gaffer. I learned the words that work,
and how to say nowt when Ivan leaned from the cab,
yelled 'Alright darling' then muttered 'Oh, it's a bleerk'.

I scowled to fit in with the younger ones.
The days dragged, cut by breaks to read *The Sun*
back in the cab, to keep out of the sun.

I was only Agency, and of course they knew.
Glazzer (from Glasgow), ex-hooligan Atkins diet Daz,
cornered me at break, asked 'What do you do?'

'English degree and that' I said, putting on Lincoln.
'Kinell', went Daz, now fine-tuning a rolly
for Glazzer, then one for himself. We didn't speak again.

Later that day, heaving boxfuls of paperbacks,
desk-chairs, or bubble-wrapped frames, we half-locked eyes,
raised brows. Then, finished early, I stood in the back,

runt of that litter, all the way to the depot past Wragby,
behind the upturned tail-lift, like a horse,
watching the tape of road rewind before me.

iii. Cold Calling

I'd just discovered Larkin's droll precision,
which meant too much: I lived with indecisions.
The day my mate got sacked for going off script
('D'y'want any windows? Nah? Okay, thanks, bye')
I started on in-stores, learning to 'target grannies'
with talk of soffits, wood-effect, safety lights,
the cost of wasted heat, 0% APR,
and other things I hadn't known were things
until I was 'self-employed' and on commission
in the doors of Asda. Red Bull gave me wings
and strings of knock-backs kept me on the ground.
'Best ignore', said Pat, our head of team,
who spunked his earnings on watches, phones and cars
and weekend clubbing, living a sort of dream
I couldn't share and learned I could've shared
if only I had cared. Or hadn't cared.

iv. Presentations

"'If no one has *misjudged* himself. Or *lied*."
  That's how it *ends*. And note the full stop, *there*.'
(I jab at it.) 'He sections off the *truth*,
  and that's because he's *really more aware* –
"the *less* deceived".' Pause. 'Thanks for listening.'

A peal of small dry claps ekes to a stop
  before I've found my seat. 'Er, thank you, er,
Rory. Now it's Lynette Johnson-Cox
  on queering Dobby in Rowling's *Harry Potter...*'.
I know it didn't go well, that Dr Pank

is less deceived than anyone else in here,
  that I misjudged myself, that in row eight
and sitting on her hands, and pencil-skirted
  (legs a helix, eyes averted), Kate
was not impressed. She whispers to her mate

as Lynette mumbles into her quivering notes
  and Pank looks on encouragingly. One day
I'd like to do her job, but know I won't.
  Then Si presents on Rochester, just to say
Her hand, her foot, her very look's a cunt,

that *t* a public schoolboy's confident click,
  and Kate is giggling now. I've got a girlfriend,
of course I have, but she's in Lampeter,
  doing Nursing. I'll call her when this ends,
to share I-love-yous as Kate and Si share a beer.

CURRICULUM REFRESH

for and about Dr Bob Pintle
Senior Lecturer in Professional Creativity, Peterborough University

The 'Equality and Inclusion' process didn't go so well
    for Pintle, when his reading list was scanned.
They said '*The Waste Land* stinks of whitest malest privilege,
    v. is four-letter fury, and should be banned,
and *Briggflatts* is a work of heteronormativity.
    The gender balance is not what we demand –
that's also triggering. All those in favour, do jazz hands, please'.

At least I'm not in Shakespeare Studies or Old and Middle English,
    he thinks, as he stands scanning rows of spines
for anyone whose name he can't pronounce, or has dismissed.
    'I know my subject, and everything was fine.'
The library's like a crèche at play-time. 'It's discrimination!
    There'll never be a course including *mine*',
he mutters, and snatches a dog-eared copy of Carol Ann Duffy's *The Bees*.

FINAL YEARS

for and about Dr Bob Pintle
Senior Lecturer in Professional Creativity, Peterborough University

For years and years, Pintle blew annual dust
off turgid lectures, was happy to earn his crust
from gobbets he'd once committed to memory –

but now the culture's changed. His new VC
has various agendas: 'Globalisation'
(foreign students), 'Employability'

and, just for him, a new 'Professionalisation
of Writing' module, whatever the fuck that is.
So he stands in front of the solemn three (of seven)

who've made it in – his class starts at 11 –
and mocks up cover letters, draws up lists,
talks up blind hopes. Of course, they'll never climb

the slippery pole rubbed dry for nepotists,
nor learn the wits to avoid it: in twelve months' time,
he knows he'll write them each a teaching-course reference

('Harry's sometimes punctual, and shows deference
to blind authority, often reads enough
to write his essays', and other copy/paste guff)

after they've all grown bored with growing bored.
'What do I need to do to get a First?'
blares Lara, as six eyes sharpen on his eyes

in sudden wakefulness. He's not rehearsed
a valid and honest answer, so he lies,
then circles the words 'Career aims!' on the board

and starts a mind map. It grows a couple of arms:
'Uni tutor' ('I'd like to do what you do'),
'Writer' ('To use my degree'). A car alarm

moans through the glass, somewhere out of view,
off campus. He lets them go. It's twenty-to.

RE: APPLICATION

FAO Dr Bob Pintle
Senior Lecturer in Professional Creativity, Peterborough University

Dear Robert,
        The Board regrets to inform
several colleagues, including you,
that your recent sabbatical applications
will not go forward, after review.

The panel felt that 'Write some poems
I haven't yet written, so it's absurd
to say much else' lacked requisite rigour.
We do ask for 'No more than 2000 words'

but suitable answers require something close.
We advise you attend our 'Winning Support for
Sabbaticals Workshop', when places are open.
There are none at present. We'll advertise more

when we secure funding. To raise an objection,
write to your Sub-Dean of Sub-Research. State
your grounds for appeal, in accordance with Guideline
11 6 2 (*Staff Handbook*, page 8).

Ensure your 4* REF Output Agreement
and book contract are both attached to the email,
with endorsements from two Student Reps and your Mentor,
and a piece of your heart. Should your first appeal fail,

we invite fresh applications each year,
though from March 2020 all will be screened
for written support from Lead Industry Partners
linked to our Strategy Goals. We are keen

to support your research. We value team players
and wish you every success going forward.
Lastly, I'm pleased, on a personal note,
to congratulate you on your Teaching Award

(Bronze). Our Faculty Press Team will write
a blog post next week, and request you take part
in our new poster ad, so congratulations!
Yours,
Dr Jim Jones
Dean, School of Arts

RE: RE: APPLICATION

FAO Dr Jim Jones
Dean of Arts, Peterborough University

Hi Jim, Bob pecks, then deletes. *Dear Jim, Oh YES!*
I'll write with that! Those sabbaticals: who got them?
And have those colleagues had thirteen precious years
on what you term 'the front line'? Anyway, Cheers!
When I find time, I'll thank you in a poem,
and place it in the fucking TLS.

I see you proclaim in your email signature line
you're 'often abroad and send out-of-hours emails,
but rarely expect instant replies to them.'
Well, Jim, tonight I marked till 10pm:
Rhetoric essays. I'd give your email a Fail,
you shite-backfilled and heaving cliché-mine.

On a personal note, how are the kids, you knob?
See much of them? Does Nanny wipe their arses?
And what are the call girls like out in Guangdong?
He sighs. Holds backspace till all his work is gone.
The cursor blinks along with his catharsis,
and he stabs *Dear Jim, That's excellent! Thanks. Bob.*

for Lloyd Pettiford and Adam Tocock

The pitch is white where the sun's not been seen
on its hill-cresting flight. The tea queue is long
and shrouded in breath, as men in fat coats
grunt at each other, though the game's going on –
but I'm on the terrace, with 64 others,
where a bloke in a tank-top and built like a tank
turns to the dug-outs and breaks the near-silence:
'Cheynge it up, Billeh boy – we're fukkin' wank!'
Then he faces the game again, squinting upfield
as one of their wingers slaps a long cross
out for a throw-in. 'C'mon lads!' he bellows,
rub-rubbing his hands.
                    So, this loss is his loss,
and also his triumph. He boos at the whistle,
says 'See yer' to others, and runs for a piss,
and doesn't drive home, cross a ground off his list,
and know he was no-one. No. He lives for this.

VERGINA SUNS

We'd set off south, across the border,
and entered another fenced-off plot

of former vias, basilicas, atriums
bordered with mosaic knots –

and cricket-static in stagnant heat:
too much, and little. We left, and found

a coffee stall selling freddocinos,
the vendor kicking a ball around

with kids and a mutt. He tried his English
with un-English zeal while we waited:

'Nottingeham Forest. Your Queeen. Your Brrexit.'
I hadn't yet reciprocated

when suddenly he jabbed at my chest
and drew my eye to what I'd bought –

my knock-off Македонија shirt –
this last morning there, as a last thought.

'Why this?' *I've been in the country of
Macedonia*, I said, with care.

'Get a PAOK shirt! Take that off!
That insults Greeks everywhere

my friend. I hate to say of a country –
"Macedonia" is liars'

whispered the Macedonian
from the Greek town of Skopia,

narrowing his eyes. 'What do
you think of this whole situation?'

He gave me change. Gap-tooth-smiled. Nodded
encouragement. *Well, the nation*

of Macedonia, of course...
I changed tack. *Mate, I really don't know.*

I'm not from here, am I? I pleaded.
I do see what you're saying, though.

Did I? But that was all he needed.
Two Germans came, which let us go.

2018

BRATISLAVA NOCTURNE

Sleet hunches us. The bars are shutting. He turns,
grinning, gloved hand stretched. 'You boys want club?
18 euros for all you like to drink!'
We shrug – why not? – and nod. He leads us down
a flight of cracked steps, along a passage, to
a pleathered lair, then leaves. There's no time to think

before the surly hostess takes our cash,
and seats us with two beers, and Slivovicas
we haven't ordered. 'Please drink!', she pleads. We do,
and bam! two more arrive. 'Please drink!', she pleads.
What is this place? The seats are oddly wide –
enough, almost, for two each side of the table –

and face a spotlit stage. It has a pole
and soon, on that, a woman who is a Pole,
I come to learn, when she crams next to me,
all cold and sparkling flesh, demanding I down
the spirit she offers. 'I here one day', she says.
'You pay me private dance?' 'No! But what

would *you* keep?' She stares. Repeats her line. Us boys
stand to leave. The floor bucks as she reaches
to squeeze my hand. Our hostess blocks the way:
'You buy farewell drink now for lovely lady.
50 each.' Two bouncers hover. We pay,
then turn to face the darkened bars, the sleet.

EASTERBUNNY

You'll never see it, as it is
invisible to the ever-more-naked eye
in any salted sky into which
we can gawp at three million years
of nothing doing. But fifty times
farther than the Sun, small enough
to rest like a golf ball on a tee
in Lake Huron, there's Makemake,
codenamed Easterbunny,
like a mission. Look it up, but not yet –
let me tell you. Imagine an egg
smashed in a crackling skillet.
Imagine a spindled squab of light
is a cryogenic ball. Or imagine
looking up Halley's Comet,
learning you'll never see it.

THE WEB

The only words I heard the old dear
sputter at John's house were *Get them*
Moslems off the telly. It shot a poison of fear
through me, more than those righteous
men I'd hardly noticed in the corner,
swinging an effigy from a pole, behind

WE WILL KILL RUSHDI APOSTATE.
They were for something called Islam
somewhere called Bradford. Somewhere.
I see her now, squeezing her little stick,
hands veined like a road atlas,
stockings bunched, body surrendering

behind a drooping Red Nose Day nose as
we play at fighting Optimus Prime and Starscream
by the hearth. Click-clack. Then that summer
as Khomeini convulsed towards Jannah I slid on water
hosed on plastic across their yard, with the
beaming sister who'd be my first wet dream.

Where *is* John now? Okay, I'll look him up.
A jaundiced new-born scrunches her face: 'Amelia
arrived! 9lbs at birth. Mummy n Daddy well
happy. Love to all! XX'. A distant Lincoln City
'At Wembo!' Chest-high in webbed water,
arms round his – wife? – who kisses him. Then

'There's no – such – thing', shouts the little man
whose videos John now posts on Facebook
with dubious zeal, 'as a "Muslim area"',
in a mainly Muslim area, where none come out.
A link below hurls my flag at me,
then the 'Jihadist cunt' awaiting sentencing:

'Sharia must come here in UK', he intones,
'and will, by choice or force. There is no need
for man-made law. And in prison I will
convert the *kuffaar*.' 'But. But
don't you think…' the reporter asks for
most of us, head dipped to the side,

pushing her notes farther across her knees;
and you already know how this ends.
A few weeks of Pot Noodles after
his early release from Belmarsh – section 20,
GBH – a wayward lad we once knew
shaved his year-old beard, made a bacon roll,

found his friends, was convicted for robbery,
regrew the beard, got out, was bought
a flight. He once made Lego trains
with a tiny solemn boy who did not know
how to want to be a girl.
Her profile meme proclaims 'Free Palestine',

across Israeli bulldozers clearing plots.
A link from her Amnesty link shows Hamas forces
attending to a supplicant, sweat-marks ghosting
the face beneath the sack. Another click and I learn
Mahmoud Ishtiwi's name. And no, I do not mean
she hasn't got a point, should know, or can't.

A tall-short double-jag stabs at where
crossed beams might once have flared on metal
or, moaning through the moon-white air,
a low Lancaster strained homeward again.

Among the sixty-thousand tool-cut names,
the sixty-thousand mechanical absences,
you find your grandfather's unobtrusive name
then step to the tree-guard-studded perimeter.

Horses put out to grass perform
a task they could not fathom.
The city beyond gets in your face,
its sixty-thousand hidden,
the cathedral crown improbably close,
atop its future barrow, or midden.

OPERATION MONDSCHEINSONATE AT
COVENTRY TRANSPORT MUSEUM

*'If the spirit which the citizens of Coventry showed on the night of
November 14th 1940 can be re-born in the hearts of our people today,
then we shall indeed see the fruits of peace.'*
Princess Elizabeth, 1948

Improbable cycles at the entrance:
a frame carved a bit like a horse;
penny farthings stretching
above the 'safety cycles';

a trike with a tiny wheel
set at the back, as if
to face-plant its decorous rider –
until someone had

the obvious epiphany.
Then the first diamond frames;
then heavy motorcycles;
then the aristocrats' and doctors'

bonneted cabriolets,
their angry grilles shining
between button-eye lamps.
Then the War to End All Wars:

a map shows how the factories
abutted their city –
Singer, Siddeley-Deasy,
Rudge-Whitworth, Rover,

Riley, Daimler, Triumph –
where cars gave way to planes
or shells, lathes grinding all night,
and men to 'factory girls'.

Then democratisation:
slim upright saloons
laid in lines behind lines
of rope and little signs.

We progress from then towards now.
And after the sleek rows
of 1930s corvettes
streamlining to elsewheres

an old couple quietly bypasses
the Blitz Experience:
teetering wax men
in ARP saucer-helmets,

stencilled DANGER
by heaps of plastic mud,
corrugated tin
throwing back each

flash and studio bang,
Pathé recordings of
Heinkel 111s overhead.
How can you imagine?

A marker flare clinks against
a warehouse roof. Another.
Then it starts in waves
as Loftflotte 3

unloads, returns to France,
reloads, wails back, unloads;
light beams track forlornly
from a city left to burn:

A huge ball of fire
shot into the air.
The whole of the roof caved in,
dragging the four men with it.

A Home Guard sat dazed,
one arm torn off. Groans guided
us to two firemen,
one with all limbs missing,

the other with his stomach
hanging out and no limbs.
I vomited, crawled away
and lay with my head in the gutter.

We gathered what remains we could find
and laid them under the trees.
One bomb hit a shelter
and muffled screams could be heard…

The boards hold just enough
to show what was, then was:
the town half-rendered to piles
cut by jagged walls,

the cathedral an urban Rievaulx,
Churchill solemnly walking
the nave unlike so many
before. And after. Then Holy

Trinity hiding its Doom,
lonely among what was –
lonely now among
what is. The factories

to be brought alive again
'defiantly'. A withered man
and two marauding grandkids
push past towards what he made

and I follow to the 1950s,
its solid Hillmans and Triumphs
shining as on a forecourt
pricelessly stolen.

II.

Love – any love – reveals us in our nakedness, our misery, our vulnerability, our nothingness.

CESARE PAVESE

(translated by Alma Elizabeth Murch)

But warm, eager, living life – to be rooted in life – to learn, to desire, to feel, to think, to act. This is what I want. And nothing less. That is what I must try for.

KATHERINE MANSFIELD

WHERE TO BUILD

I never thought I'd have a home
but then I'd built one up from the bay,
a shrub-scrubbed cleft half-hiding it,
a plunging stream behind the grate

and locals pointed up, or down,
to where I lived beside myself
for years, with all I'd wanted most,
building a greenhouse, annexe, shelves,

and made it all I knew to want
and drowned the voice that said I don't
with all I'd always done for this
and grew tomatoes, seed to light

and ate them, happily, every night,
and fixed the leak that drew the rain
and fixed it when it sprung again.
Well, I knew of rock across the bay –

a skerry? – green-topped, curving round
to out of sight behind near rock.
But rain set in, the endless rain,
and through the sheet of endless cloud

a jet of sudden light cracked down
across that further hunk of land,
which glimmered ginger. And it stayed
for seconds, minutes, hours, days,

the whole life of my house away.

'Ultimately, and precisely in the deepest and most important matters,
we are unspeakably alone; and many things must happen, many things
must go right, a whole constellation of events must be fulfilled, for one
human being to successfully advise or help another.'
   Rainer Maria Rilke, translated by Stephen Mitchell

...in person with someone else, or by phone with me?
Phone, please: you can't commit to one time or place.
You're taking positive steps now. Relief! And yes
it looks like you are and then that marker slips
behind sun-blocking trees while you walk on.
No, you're taking positive steps. *Write it all down*:
one thing on one side, the other on the other
until each proliferates: two jig-sawing trees
joined at the roots, the subterranean nub.

*

Picture somewhere you love. A wood. *Who's there,*
with you in the wood? Who has been there before
so often. Who wants to be there most?
But what do you want? The trees.
No trees. The trees. No trees. The trees.

*

It isn't about advice, but finding your own way.
After this, we have two more sessions.
                              What will you do?
You don't know and can't and begin to explain.
That's 30 minutes over again.
And today I want to leave you with this...

*

Who is she? That isn't why you're here. She's a voice,
just a voice, as you stare into hedges yards from the house.
She is hedges and walls and sky and a voice.
...*because of course this can't go on*. It does and can't.
Go away on your own. You don't know anywhere else.

*

The trees are still and thick with maturation. Write it down.
A gap – and hills hide the horizon. Write it down.
The ground is bare patches, dust-bathing birds. Write it down.
Does where you go reveal what you are? Write it down.
Tomorrow is today is yesterday and won't be. Write it down.
You tell her this. *Write it down.*

HAD AND HELD

i. Last Night

'It can't work, then.' Relief dulled by two cheap bottles
forced us asleep that last time, side by side
with space for the others we might soon enough pray to meet –

to wake at the shock of held hands, too rare, too late,
and edge back to our sides. Your feet poked out
as I rose, blessed by hangover, new-headed,

to brush my teeth, smooth my hair, remove my few things
from your fan-cooled bedsit, my wife, and stare at you
with love as you stared back with love and closed the door.

ii. Self-Storage

It's nine months since we crammed all we'd accrued
from shells to shelving, pots to postcards, somewhere
here, in case we 'worked it out'. But where?

He squints at the screen. 'Unit...two-eleven,
third corridor. You moving house?' We pause
the same pause. 'Yes', I say. 'Something like that.

We don't know where...'. She shoots a marital glance,
as if to say I've gone too far again,
and curls a hand round her waist: our neat black diamond –

unusual enough – is off it now. 'So, pull
the vans right up to the ledge: the doors slide over',
he says, gliding one arm across the other.

We never saw it coming; he's seen it before.
'Good luck.' We smile, and then offload our lives
in ordered halves. I can't write that part down.

It didn't happen. This desk proves otherwise.

iii. The Ring

Taking it off was also a ceremony,
but masqueraded as a non-event.
It crushed the locking knuckle, then sped free,
leaving a bleached band. In time, that went,
and looked quite normal. But feels much as it did,
heavy with all it means forever. Meant.

iv. Last Home

If I could only close my eyes harder   *I don't mean to try or try to be*
our demijohn would still be in its nook,   *full of murky promises*
our albums stacked beneath the coffee table,   *you still might but can't stand to see*
and you'd be coiled on the sofa with a book   Wide Sargasso Sea? *It is*
as I came in, finding space on my hook   *one is 'Hers', the next is 'His'*

for coat and scarf. You'd raise your eyes, and look   *and I am running late again*
less wearied in the picture above your head –   *glaring through the one-way glass*
me holding you, the one my Best Man took   *raised to the eye, put down again*
before he fucked our host's girl in her bed,   *glaring through the one-way glass*
and after our unmade promises were said.   *glaring through the one-way glass*

THE POLLYANNA PRINCIPLE

Former RAF Woodhall Spa Nature Reserve

The runway ran its barren mile of asphalt
then gave where a gravel pit had stolen the end:
a swan sailed like a model, bank to bank
then halfway back again,

and water boatmen stop-started at the edge.
Two mallards winged across, wheeled over the reeds,
engaged their stubby-footed landing gear,
and yapped for scraps or seed

we hadn't brought. There was little else round there
but darkening sky, then the hungry alarm of thunder.
She nodded at our dot of car – 'Shall we?' –
then marched downrange. I always followed her.

'Fuck you, I won't do what you tell me. Fuck you...'.
You'd never danced to this before, like this,
with a doe-eyed goth in Docs. Now, you were in luck,
cheek to cheek and groin to groin. You kissed,
then felt each other up behind the hall,
and waved her off when she got picked up by her mum.
So, do you call? Play cool? The next morning you called:
'Doin' much?' 'Nuf'n'.' 'I'm goin' town. Wanna come?'

A few years passed. You both had bills to pay
with new careers, and a mortgaged duplex in Maidstone,
so you went to Crete on a package holiday:
the last before your first, though if you'd known...
You had your Game Boy Advance and *Big Mutha Trucker*s
to fill the long longueurs; her headphones fizzed:
'I won't do what you tell me. Motherfucker',
which might have been nice to share, but what now is?

More years have gone. Her parents, too. You've moved
to Gravesend for a post at Gravesend Heating
and Lighting Solutions. The wedding snaps have improved
with the sheen of impossible choices, impossible meetings,
and peel a little from clip-frames along the hall.
Tonight, your lad has his college leavers' ball,
and whispers sweet nothings in his girlfriend's ear.
They're the sweetest nothings she'll ever hear.

OLD FLAT, ABANDONED

I force open the door:
its shadow shoots
down the wall
where webs tremble
in door-breath and light.
A thread bows. Breaches.
Ahead, the flight
of (bare wood) steps
(with carpet tacks)
runs up to gloom.

So, I've come (back)
to find (my) room;
each step misstepped
as I trod lightly
to where I reach
for those misspent nights
when shadow trembled
down that wall
until one (lost) boot
kicked shut the door.

HUNDREDS OF LITTLE LANTERNS

'He's pleased to meet you underneath the horse
In the cathedral with the glass stained black
Singing sweet high notes that echo back.'
     Elliott Smith

They don't belong under these leaf-tied bosses,
proliferating arches, dark illumined windows
smirched in light: two of the few hundred, checked

by ceremony, clutching unlit candles and an Order of Service
('To be a Light: A Special Festive Service with Lantern Parade
And Lighting of the Cathedral Christmas Tree')

as, arrayed far beneath the crossing, one white-robed body,
all synchronised little faces and tremulous heads, reaches
its sure finale, then dematerialises into kids. Some infants

aloft in the nave cry out hearts in fugue, while they can;
then she turns to page four of twelve as the Dean reappears:
'Light your candles, which symbolise the Light.'

And she stays head to his shoulder, gladly refusing to sing
but singing in him through hand to still-ringed hand,
or a clash of eyes to steady too-eager song.
What is this? It's as right as anything, and Wrong.

You needn't ask why I fall silent – *and not like this snow*, you said.
But accepting what I am, and what I'm not
you lead me over cranial cobbles
showing through the slush,
past rich shadows
where saints
gawp from a
church-front,
the baubled tree,
three steamy, chattering bars,
then out of Old Town, past the CUNT
sprayed as if to remind me, a breadcrumb to home,
and up to our Ghetto hotel. Quick through the lobby. To bed.

ONE-PARENT FAMILIES (Sheldon Press, 1979)

'A comprehensive guide' – Mother & Baby

Was it? Each dog-ear, thin spine-crack
opens on our time refracted
along the unchartable ways we acted;
and Dad, at court then, to win me back,

but doomed, would've bristled at the name
which drew you to it, desperate to learn –
who, clearing out, hands it to Age Concern,
crammed in a bag, for someone the same.

LIKE FATHER

Started 2000, finished 2019
For W. C.

My daddy was Irish and famous – 'Well, sort of Irish
and sort of famous', he said – and told the truth.
He loved and he was loved, and was a joker,
        and in his youth

he'd passed the eleven-plus with such high marks
they'd sent him to private school (plush lawns, straw hats)
but then he'd felt 'oppressed by the Oxbridge conveyor'
        so that was that

for years, while he wrote in garrets and took 'real jobs':
porter on Jersey, bank clerk. He explored
the world, and then read English up at Leicester,
        then at Oxford,

and won awards, and 'found' he was getting in print,
but still worked summers at Leicester station goods-yard.
'Am I as bright as you, Daddy?' 'Probably not'.
        So it was hard

not to pine for all he represented
on access visits, and not to be beguiled,
but I knew I wasn't as special, that I was
        an anxious child

who liked to play with marbles on his own,
while mum cooked, watched EastEnders, tidied up.
Who teachers said should 'come out of his shell'.
        Who had a pup

and made her his best friend, and got in trouble
for daydreaming, and caused too much of a fuss
about his distant dad. Who scrapped. Who failed
       the eleven-plus

and went to a comprehensive where he learned
never to try too hard. Who knew his place
was in the middle. Who watched his lurch-drunk father
       jab at the face

of a steadfast woman patently too good
to stay with him. (She didn't.) Who wouldn't become
a poet and scholar too, or much at all:
       he was too dumb.

Who later found the custody hearing documents
while helping his mother clear her musty attic:
the affidavits of all his dad's ex-lovers,
       each emphatic

that *I'm sure the child's interests are best served*
by being kept from this abusive man,
a drunk who bullied and hit me; his arrest statement
       from when my Nan

lost her front teeth (I hadn't been told the reason).
Until then, I'd seen one short, partial report
to which my father had clung. Mum had buried
       most retorts,

and Nan was now in her functional little urn.
And I was trying to be like him – a bit,
in fewer and fewer ways – and started a poem
       and this is it.

EPITHALAMIUM: POSTSCRIPT AND PROLEPSIS

He's in love with being in love
but how much love is left to give
at 78? She's 46,
newly arrived, and here to live:

he's signed to her his full devotion
and terraced house. Now he sits
alone all day in a tiny room
he used to only sleep in. It's

a refuge. She sleeps where his office was
on a single mattress he acquired
then busies herself: this kitchen needs
stripping, then the yard. She's tired.

She fends off calls: 'No here, he sleepink'
she says a few times every day,
to grainy voices down the phone
who'd called to chat chess, poetry

or football, or later just to see
if anything might be done, or said.
She must negotiate, alone,
her GP, bank: he stays in bed.

And this is love – and then was love.
She grieves, sells up, then moves away
to where her folks can help; his son,
who only used to come to stay

when work allowed, won't bother her now.
Then one warm night she Google-translates
this poem, and smiles. Its implications
mean more than she can navigate.

LOSERS; WINNERS

'A small boy clambering up stadium steps for the very first time, gripping
his father's hand, gawping at that hallowed stretch of turf beneath him
and, without being able to do a thing about it, falling in love.'
   Sir Bobby Robson

So up those steps and out to scrambled senses:
Subbuteo men on baize, surrounded by heads
and hoardings, spurts of smoke, occasional hollers.
It's all so far away, all takes so long.
You've just turned seven. You know most of the rules

and never can wear that Liverpool shirt again
though Nan scrimped for it two long months ago.
No, now you're in the South Stand, Carrow Road,
Ray Houghton's been upended by Ian Crook,

and you are jeering, because the others are jeering,
and hugging your father's suddenly fatherly arm,
and waving the new inflatable canary
you'll later clothe, then pierce, and finally lose.

You lost. But now you're Norwich, so Dad is too:
you'll take the jokes and jibes for him at school
from glory-hunters in Arsenal and Liverpool shirts,
while he's at home five hundred miles from you.

★

And now he's purblind, and ransacked from thirty more years
of self-made battles: black-eyed women leaving,
and blackout drinking, then all those bottomless days
of pining for chances. That radiation scar
like chicken skin is not his fault. Nor the fear.

But what of the new young wife who's stopped being here,
yet suddenly owns his house, and all he had?
You scowl when people say he got what was coming.
And you're with his friend 'to tell your father the truth' –

not your idea, the friend's, who's cooked a lunch.
The three of you sit in cutlery-squeaking silence,
then two find the heart to try. And when it's no use
there's cheesecake, and Norwich on the radio.

That static as Teemu Pukki skips a defender
and finds the net is ten thousand hims and yous
applauding the way you couldn't those years ago.
You watch his eyes. He sees the same things you do.

DEFENCES

Kirby Muxloe Castle

Crikey! you say. *It's gorgeous!* Across the moat
two hunks of unfinished battlement reflect,
a bit like the butterfly prints we once did at school:
the bottom halves faint and blemished. *Let's walk it round,*
and never mind the scuppered portaloo
breaching by the bridge that was a drawbridge:
the teams of mallards sifting wavelets don't.
Then when you see a moorhen padding the roots
of an undercut willow – instinctive bird-brained head
quantum-leaping about on the stem of her neck,
ten balls of chick bunching and stretching behind
as she pushes away to the safety of open water –
you act as I once would've. *Look! She's got 10!*

At Belfast Zoo, between goes on the toddler swing,
I finger-jabbed at a peacock stretching its fan:
Duck! But I was one and can't remember
this tale which might be true. And ten years later,
a 'Young Ornithologist' tied to the heart of his father,
keen to impress somehow, as we boated the Broads'
long bends of reed-furred river, blue-green-blue,
I pointed out a preening crested grebe
riding the ripples. He was half-blind by then,
a sudden genetic inconvenience,
and couldn't see it and said he thought he could.
A windmill stretched its X across the sky,
geese beat frantic along the water-runway
(he turned his head to show me I could show him)
and that night when we'd moored beside The Swan,

and after my bedtime, as I raced model hawks
surreptitiously around my cabin
he punched his would've-been wife in the eye
then went back to his scotch. I watched them through
the crack he couldn't discern along the door-jamb,
and knew the truth, then how to doubt the truth
when he said – then when she said – that she'd slipped:
the bitterness of justice

                    never done.
Dandelions are stitched down to the water,
where ramsons have flowered. I pick one and we taste;
you bunch your nose to wrinkles – do you mean it? –
then pounce for another bite. Lead me behind
this blackthorn hedge. No, let me drive us home.

CHILDE BEHAR'S INTENDED PILGRIMAGE

'Morn dawns; and with it stern Albania's hills...'
Lord Byron, Childe Harold's Pilgrimage

Our porter Behar's village crams a pass,
lidded by this great mitre of new hotel
for rich Albanians. Doubled in its glass,
an EU flag lops, widens. Time will tell.
The birds have started, as everywhere; personnel
arrive to make us breakfast, as everywhere;
the kitchen vent breathes pork and pastry smells.
Your swimsuit is stretched like a cat on the balcony chair
as you wake and groan conscious, still here, still not quite anywhere.

So, morn dawned. With it, stern Albania's hills
grew ridges down to dark, convulsive streams.
At check-out, Behar, half a child still,
offers a cigarette, and shares his dreams:
'Here we have US lottery. It means
if you win, you get Green Card like Americans.
My brother did, now I'll go!' 'Where?' He beams.
'Detroit. That place has many Albanians...'.
I bet. We pass him our keys. He nods and shakes our hands.

THEY STILL LEAP OVER THE STRID

She skips in front, then pins her feet like a soldier
at drill, and points. 'So *here's* the Strid', a stride
beyond her stride, and air comes from it, colder
than it is, perhaps, and down this six-foot-wide

breach in bedrock, those who slipped and died
felt its oil-slick skin, its pull, each boulder
beneath the imperfect glass. So when you tried
to stop me leaping, I stopped, knowing I'd
grown older.

GARLIC

i. Wimbledon Men's Final, 1994

His winners were yours, the future flung off, flung off, flung off
like the lines of rain from your balding Slazenger ball
when it clipped each puddle you'd airbrushed from your mind.

Yes, you were Nothingtown, Lincolnshire's swarthy Yank,
every diamond hole in the fence an imagined face – where
this court gave over to weeds, here and there, until the asphalt

is ruts, and runnels of weed, and that's when you return,
no scuffed racquet over your shoulder, and no one to plonk back
your sliced backhands. It's been – what? – twenty years

since you were last here with nothing to show but the bluster
you'd never felt. One dead net-post remains, its crank handle
jammed with rust, the fattened threads shining freshly

after you butt it with a palm. You can name the bindweed now,
but don't have to live with it. What else to do but know
you needn't have come, that it might repeat on you like garlic?

ii. It Might Repeat on You

'Garlic!', she play-screams. And Christ it's been less than a year
since she'd never known it and now she wants pesto to dribble
on pizzas, the frontierswoman pleasure of knowing We Made

This, as it turns to rot in a back-of-shelf Kilner jar this winter.
She's already ripping the waxy green ears from their stems,
feeding them into a bag, playing gleaner. But she has made

you the gleaner, hasn't she? This warmth comes and goes
like a nuzzly cat. You bend and detach a buoyant flowerhead,
and nibble off budding flowers like they're redcurrants.

A woodpecker's nutting his way home in salvos, somewhere,
and when she asks what it is you mustn't laugh. She's
irritated now, backpalming a hip, staring across this edible lawn:

why aren't you helping? So you start, swift at each clump, gladly
nudged back to the instant as she knows to see it, in this acre
of woodpecker echoes, making a job where he has his.

NOTTINGHAM NOCTURNE

Another Friday night.
A mile or so away
a boy will be watching
chunks of kebab dribble
mouth to paving
down a pissy alley.
He doesn't know
we've all been him,
and it wouldn't help.

Some are working
night shifts, some are
alone, always more
are cocooned in doors,
at least until daybreak;
and you are restless
beside rest, beside
recharging, remoulding
desires, as the sycamore
heaves in the lamplight.

Do not pretend
you have done all
you could for anyone.
And try not to breathe
too loud, and listen
as she snores rabbit snores
against you, and rainbursts
crackle on glass.
Never stop listening.

ACKNOWLEDGEMENTS

Thanks are due to the editors of the following, in which several of these poems first appeared, sometimes in earlier versions: *Ambit*, *The Compass*, *The High Window*, *New Statesman*, *PN Review*, *Poetry Review*, *The Times Literary Supplement* and *Wild Court*. I am also grateful to Alan Jenkins, Anjna Chouhan, Nicholas Friedman and William Ivory for providing feedback, and to my editor, Michael Schmidt, and Andrew Latimer at Carcanet. The quotations in 'Operation Mondscheinsonate at Coventry Transport Museum', some of which have been slightly altered, are from Ron Vice, *We Re-invented the Wheel* (Dunlop Aerospace Limited, 2003). The four poems concerning Dr Bob Pintle are warmly dedicated to Dr Andrew Taylor, who did not inspire them.